Saving Stripes A Kitty's Story

JUSTIN M. ANDERSON

ISBN-13: 978-1500709112

ISBN-10: 1500709115

DEDICATION

This book is dedicated to all animal lovers, especially people like Stephanie and Shari Timberlake. The sisters opened The Adopt-A-Pet Shop in Plymouth, Minn., in 2012 with a single goal in mind: to help as many animals as possible find forever homes.

ACKNOWLEDGMENTS

Savings Stripes: A Kitty's Story, though told from the point of view of Stripes the cat, is a story that involved a lot of people. Special thanks go out to neighbors Bob, Jamie, Aaron, Calvin, Brooke, Randy and Kim K. Without their help, saving Stripes and her family would never have been possible.

My parents deserve thanks as well. My mother took the photos that appear in the book, and also helped with the story. My father did the layout for the book.

I would also like to thank the Golden Valley Animal Humane Society. The organization took in all four cats shortly after the rescue, successfully rehabilitated the kittens and got them adopted out within a week of their arrival.

As for the mother cat, Faith, the credit for her rescue goes to Stephanie Timberlake from The Adopt-A-Pet Shop in Plymouth, Minn. She stepped in to save Faith after the Animal Humane Society deemed her unadoptable.

Turns out a serious illness is the reason Faith's behavior was so unbecoming. She was suffering from pneumonia when The Adopt-A-Pet shop took her in. Stephanie took her to a vet who gave her the proper medicine. Once her health improved, she went home with Kim C. for a few months. Then on Nov. 1, 2014, Faith, like her kittens, found her forever home.

100% of the proceeds from sales of this book are being donated to The Adopt-A-Pet Shop to help support their tireless efforts to save as many cats as possible.

PROLOGUE

Knollway Park - July 27, 2014.

It was another warm sunny day at the Knollway Park in Minnetonka, Minnesota. When Faith and her kittens woke up, they were probably hopeful that something interesting would happen.

Because the park had been closed for about a month, there had not been any children to watch in a while. Faith and her kittens loved to watch the kids play and missed all the activity.

Faith, a beautiful dilute tortoiseshell cat, couldn't remember how she ended up in the park. Though it seemed to be the perfect place when it came time for her kittens to be born. There were plenty of places to hide, which was good. The babies would be safe.

The twins, Arthur and Anna, are bigger than Stripes, the third cat in the litter. Anna and Arthur both have beautiful gray-brown coats with stripes and spots on their stomachs. The best way to tell them apart is the shape of their heads. Anna's face is long and pointed. Arthur's is round.

As for Stripes, she is an orange tabby. Like her brother and sister, she has stripes, hence the name. This is Stripes' story as told from her point of view.

SAVING STRIPES: A KITTY'S STORY

By Justin M. Anderson

Anna and Arthur loved to play and wrestle. Mom always had to yell at them to slow down and not run ahead. I guess I'm more cautious in nature though and preferred to spend time close to my mother.

On that fateful day, however, when we heard a loud rumble even I ran to the edge of the forest to see where the noise was coming from. Mom yelled at us to stop, but our curiosity got the better of us and we ignored her.

When we got to the edge of the forest, we saw a big machine dump a pile of wood chips next to the park where the little humans play. A short time later more machines arrived.

The workers took turns scooping up the wood chips and dumping them around the play places in the park. All the noise was so interesting. Anna, Arthur and I couldn't resist the urge to come out of the woods and check it out.

There must have been a dozen humans in the park. We wanted to run over to them and play, but Mom warned us to stay back. I don't know why, but she seemed to be afraid of the humans.

When one of the humans came over to us, I was so excited I began to purr and roll over. She was so pretty. She had long blond hair and a very happy looking face. She said, "Here kitty, kitty," and laughed when I came over and rubbed on her leg.

She must have been very smart because she knew we were hungry. She opened a box and took out a sandwich and cut off a piece for each of us. Anna, Arthur and I devoured the sandwich. It tasted so good!

I called for Mom to come over and try the food the girl had brought, but she wasn't interested. Instead, she backed deeper into the woods.

After we had our fill, we followed Mom into the forest and curled up in the pipe we called home. It was in the middle of the forest, surrounded by plants and in the perfect place to jump out and catch food.

Later that afternoon, a neighborhood boy and his mother came into the park. I assumed they were checking on the construction progress. It was the first time we had seen a kid there in a while and we were excited.

The boy was only there a few seconds though before running off. We were sad at first, but delighted when he returned with a stick toy. He obviously wanted to play with us.

I couldn't believe it. It was the best toy ever—a stick with little strings on the end.

Anna and Arthur played with it first, and once they were done with it, I ran over and grabbed it with my teeth. I looked around and nobody was coming towards me so I ran as fast as I could, dragging the stick into the woods.

The boy was close behind though, yelling and waving his arms. I think he was saying, Stop, give it back! I was so scared. I jumped, then ran.

I wanted to bring the toy back to our hiding spot, but after it got stuck in the branches a few times, I realized I'd never make it if I didn't drop the stick. So that's what I did.

Arthur and Anna, who had been watching from behind a tree, followed me into the woods when they saw me take off. We watched from the safety of our hiding spot as the boy eventually found the stick and walked away with it.

A short time later, some more humans showed up. Mom was very suspicious. After they put a bowl filled with food at the edge of the forest, Anna and Arthur didn't hesitate. They came out of hiding, walked right up to the bowl and started eating.

I started to follow them, but something told me to hang back a bit and it's a good thing I did. A man caught them, one after another, and put them in a cage.

I wanted no part of that. I ran as fast as I could back into the woods while calling for my mother. Mom had watched the whole thing from her hiding place in the forest and began to cry. I nuzzled up to her and that's how we fell asleep.

The next day the park was quiet again. No machines. Just a few people who came with little ones to play. Mom and I went back to the spot where Anna and Arthur had been taken, and it wasn't long before the blond girl who had given us her sandwich the day before arrived with her mother. This time, they brought some food in shiny cans for us. Mom and I both ate before slipping back into the woods.

Later that evening, the same man who had caught Anna and Arthur returned. He set down a bowl and I walked right up to it. I was so hungry I couldn't help myself. I started to eat, and when I wasn't looking he grabbed me. I hissed and bit him, but still ended up in the cage. He then convinced Mom to walk into a cage he had waiting for her by putting a can of food inside. Mom hissed too, but she didn't struggle.

Once we were both in the cages we were brought to a big box that the humans seemed to live in. Then they carried us up what I later learned were stairs and reunited us.

Anna and Arthur were meowing louder than I had ever heard them meow before when Mom and I joined them in a big cage set up in the living room. I later learned it was actually a dog kennel. What is a dog?

Even though Anna and Arthur can be a pain sometimes, I sure was glad to be back with them again. I had never been so happy to see another cat in my life.

The humans turned out to be the mom and boy we had seen in the park the previous day. The dad was there too. He was very nice. He obviously had experience with cats.

The family gave us food, water and a litter box that seemed to come out of thin air. Then they played with us for a while before turning off the lights and saying goodnight.

The next morning they came back to the cage we were being kept in and gave us new food and water. They kept on taking pictures of us, which made me feel kind of special. We played and ate and then played some more.

Just when we started getting comfortable, Mom started making a racket. She could see and smell the outdoors through an open sliding door, but couldn't go outside because the wires kept her… and us… contained. She eventually calmed down and I felt better. I told her that it was okay. At least we were all together again.

It wasn't long before more food arrived. Boy, I thought, I sure can get used to this. It's so much easier when the food comes to you than when you have to hunt for it.

With our tummies full and feeling content, all three of us kittens decided it was time for a nap. Mom had settled down in the back of the cage and was lying down on her side. Anna and Arthur took that as a sign it was time to nurse. I joined them, then we all took a long cat nap.

Shortly after we woke up, our whole world was turned upside down again. Two men picked up the cage we were in and carried it out to this thing they called a car. They put the cage in the back of it and then a motor similar to the one we had heard at the park started up.

We bounced around for several minutes before coming to a stop. I didn't know if I should be scared or excited. Mom was terrified. Anna and Arthur were trying to get out. I, on the other paw, wanted to do it again.

After a few minutes of hanging out with the mom, dad and boy in the car, the cage we were in was brought inside and set down in a cold, clammy room. There were two new humans inside who bent down to check us out.

We were unsure about what to do so we just stayed in the corner of the cage, close to Mom. She didn't say a word. I started making some noise. I guess you could call them peeps. The boy came over to pet me again and I felt relaxed.

We sat in the room together for a while. Then all of a sudden the familiar people got up and left us with a stranger. It was another girl. She had long blond hair, like the girl who had given us the sandwich in the park. But she was not smiling.

She reached into the cage and grabbed Arthur. He cried out in fear, but before he could do anything to defend himself, she put him in a different cage, a smaller one. Next came Anna, and then me. She later told the humans who we had stayed with the night before that I was the feistiest of the litter.

When it came time to put Mom in a different cage, she did not go quietly. She hissed and growled and tried to scratch the girl as if her life depended on winning the fight. The girl quickly gave up and slammed the door shut on the cage. She came back into the room a few minutes later with two other people. One of them was carrying this thing they called a net.

They opened the door of the cage and put it over Mom's head before she could react. They then put her in another cage. I cried out. Actually, shrieked. But it didn't do any good.

Once all four of us were caged up, they moved us into another room. That was the last time we saw the nice humans who had let us stay at their house.

The next thing we knew, we were in a big room with all kinds of noise. There must have been 100 cats in there of all shapes, sizes and colors. Some of them were meowing loudly. Others were growling and scratching each other, but I focused on the ones that were playing and having a good time. I guess that's how I kept myself calm.

The kitten I was most interested in was a tiny little fluff ball rolling around on something that looked soft. Sure beats rolling around in the sand I thought to myself.

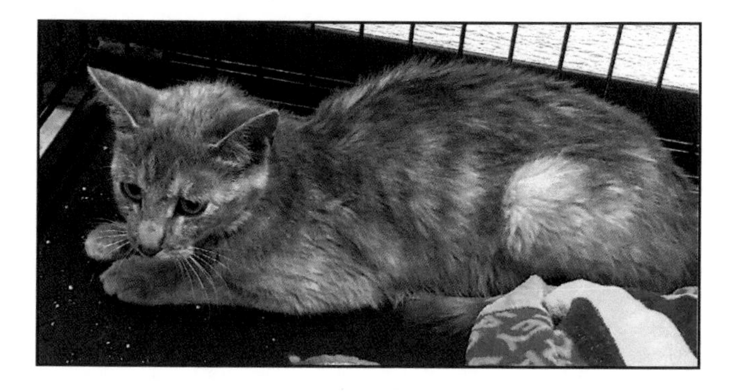

Mom was making a racket again. Her cage was right across from ours in the room. I still managed to fall asleep though. I was so tired.

The next morning, Anna, Arthur and I woke up when we felt the cage we were in swinging back and forth. It took all my strength to balance myself so I wouldn't slide backwards. Eventually, the cage was put down and once again, there were hands reaching in for us. One after another, me, my sister and brother were moved into a bigger cage. And it was filled with toys.

Once Anna, Arthur and I made ourselves comfortable in the cage, one of the humans brought over some food and water for us. It hadn't been too long since we ate, but I found myself hungry again. The food tasted so good. If I could speak their language, I would have said, "Thank you very much."

After we ate, all three of us got busy licking our fur and cleaning up. As we did that, humans we had never seen before began entering and exiting the room. I later found out they worked at the place we were at: The Animal Humane Society I'm not sure what that means, but it must be good. I feel safe and comfortable here.

We slept on and off throughout the rest of the day, and then what I assume was the next morning, the humans dressed in uniforms came back to see us. They took Anna and Arthur away and left me all by myself in the cage.

I was kind of scared, but then this nice girl came into the room and picked me up and we went to a big box, what I later learned was a room, to play. Wow, the toys in there were amazing! There were balls and sticks and things that made noise.

I had never run around so much in my life. At least I don't think I had anyway. After a while I crashed on the floor, ready for a nap. The girl picked me up and brought me back to a cage in the room with all the cats. I could see Anna and Arthur in another cage across the hall. They were out like a light!

It wasn't long before feeding time came around again. I ate the food they gave me, took a long drink, then curled up in the corner of the tiny cage and went to sleep.

The next morning I woke up to a racket. There were cats meowing and jumping around in cages. I looked up and saw the cage Arthur and Anna were in being put on a silver thing with wheels and taken away. I called out to them and Arthur meowed back, "Goodbye!"

"Goodbye?" I said quietly, not realizing at that moment what that word meant. After they disappeared from the room, it was my turn next. Only I was wheeled to a different room.

When I got there, I saw a bunch of humans wearing masks. Before I could figure out what was going on, I felt a sharp prick, then the light started fading. When I woke up, I was back in the room with all the other cats. I was pretty sore and didn't feel like getting up. I wonder what they did to me. Oh well, it couldn't have been anything too serious because I barely remember it now.

The next day, the same friendly humans who had rescued us came to the Animal Humane Society to visit me. I was so excited when I saw them walk into the room. I started purring and rubbing on the cage.

I remember thinking, I sure hope they're here to see me, and they were. One of the people in uniform opened the cage I was in and brought me to a big box that the people could fit in. The boy and his mom followed us into the box. Then, the worker put me down and I was able to run right up to them.

I couldn't believe my luck. I rubbed on the boy's ankle first, then the mom. Then ran back to the boy. There were some toys in the room, and they were tossing them around. I chased after one ball, then another. Then the people picked me up.

I was purring so loudly, I couldn't even think clearly. I just had this huge sense of joy.

We played for a while, then the girl in the uniform returned and put me back in the cage. If I could have talked, at that point I would have said, "Hey, lady! What do you think you're doing? Bring me back to the people!"

Then the nice people I was thinking about adopting came over to the cage. The boy stayed with me while the mom wandered off.

What seemed like hours later, a girl in a uniform came over and opened the cage, then put me in what I later learned was a travel cage. The boy picked it up and I was on the move. I had no idea where I was going, but anywhere was better than this scary place.

As the door opened, I looked back one more time, sensing with relief that I would probably never be back.

I thought to myself, I hope all the other cats here will find good families, and I hope my siblings got adopted by good families too. I silently wished them and my mom good luck.

It wasn't long before I found myself back in the big moving box that had brought me to the animal shelter in the first place. They buckled me in and we were off.

We drove for a while, then before I knew it we were at what was going to become my new home. The boy brought me up to his room and opened the door of the cage. I didn't know what to do first when the door opened, but instinct told me to dash under the dresser, where I stayed for a while.

Later, a boy and girl I had seen in the park when my family was rescued from the woods came to visit. They also seemed friendly. The next thing I knew, the mom came in and pulled me out from under the dresser. Then she picked me up and brought me down the stairs to a small bathroom and closed the door.

It wasn't so bad in there. I had food, water and toys, and got frequent visits from the people. I stayed in that room for a couple of days and got pretty used to it. It was kind of cozy. There was a round thing they called a sink that was nice to nap in.

Just when I had gotten used to the little room though, they relocated me again. This time to a much bigger room with what they called a window to the outside.

I could see the woods where I used to live in the distance. I do not ever want to go there again!

The next couple of days were filled with play and fun. I had a lot of toys to play with, but my favorite one to this day is the stick with the little strings on the end.

The toys were fun and all, but it wasn't long before I started wondering what it would be like to explore more of the house. At that point I was restricted to one room.

Then as if they had read my mind, one day the door slowly opened and I was able to look out. Imagine my surprise when this gray thing poked its head in the door and said, "Who are you and what are you doing here?"

I said, "I'm Stripes. You're big!"

She said, "I am Caroline. I am medium, and this is my house. You were not invited."

Caroline hissed at me and growled. I was a bit scared and said, "Why are you being so mean? I just want to play."

"No thank you," said Caroline, who then walked away.

This went on for a couple of days, while the door was kept partially open with a stringy thing they called a rubber band on it.

Caroline and I touched paws a few times through the door. After a few days, she wasn't hissing at me anymore, which was good.

Just when I was getting used to the door being partially open and getting to try to play with Caroline, the humans changed things up on me again.

They put me in the same big cage I had been in with my family when I first came, and let Caroline walk around and look at me. At first I didn't know what to do and stayed in the corner where I had been when I was with my mom, but after a while Caroline got bored and left, leaving me to explore my new surroundings. I rubbed up against a spot in the cage and was surprised to discover that I could fit through it.

I now had the ability to go anywhere in the house I wanted, and ran downstairs to find my boy. When I found him I rubbed against his leg, and he looked down with a confused look and said, "Hey, how did you get down here?"

Caroline was nearby and came running over to see what was going on and started sniffing me.

"What are you doing down here? I didn't say you could leave your cage!" she hissed.

"You're not the boss of me!" I said. "The boy named Justin is."

"You have a lot to learn kid," said Caroline. "I'm the Alpha, which means I was here first and get to decide what we do. You must return to your cage or leave at once."

Just then, the mom came out of a room with strange machines in it they call an office and scooped up Caroline, who shouted, "How dare you! Put me down at once."

Justin picked me up next. "Whoa!" I said. "I've been lifted again!"

Justin brought me back to the cage, which I immediately escaped from again. He was watching this time though so my secret was revealed.

When the dad came home, they surprised me by putting Caroline in the cage and letting me explore the house. You'll never believe this, but Caroline seemed to like it in the cage. She even rolled around in the litter box. How yucky!

I asked her what she was doing and she said, "Nothing! Now go away."

She still to this day likes to roll around in the big litter box downstairs. I always ask her what she is doing and she says, "Nothing. Go away!"

It took a few weeks before we were both allowed to have free run of the house. I was locked up in the big extra bedroom at night while Caroline got to explore the house.

During the day I stayed downstairs with the mom in the office. Caroline stayed upstairs. Then when the dad came home, all the doors would be open and Caroline and I would be allowed to spend time together. We did the best we could to ignore each other.

One day while I was relaxing on the big bed and taking a nap, Caroline jumped up and grabbed me. I was so shocked I didn't know what to do. "Get off my bed!" she growled.

"It's not your bed," I said. "It's the people's bed. I'm sure they would like us to both hang out up here with them and be buddies. I've heard them say that a few times."

"We are not buddies!" exclaimed Caroline.

"Oh yes we are," I thought. "Oh yes we are!"

EPILOGUE

By Rachel M. Anderson

It took several months before Caroline and Stripes finally settled into a routine and began acting more like siblings than enemies. Now they spend their days playing, eating, and of course hanging out as much as they possibly can with their people.

As for Stripes' mother, Faith, a few days after the kittens were adopted, the Animal Humane Society deemed Faith feral and unadoptable, so with her life on the line, I called Stephanie Timberlake at The Adopt-A-Pet Shop in Plymouth, Minn. She said, "Let's get her out of there! We'll find her a home."

We paid the Animal Humane Society's fee for having housed the cat for a week and brought Faith home for safe keeping until Stephanie could pick her up. Since we had an out-of-town trip planned that week, our neighbors, the Almen-Yakes, the people who had helped catch the cats in the first place, took Faith for the rest of the week. (At that time her name was Maddie, selected by Brooke Almen-Yake.)

When Stephanie picked her up and got her to a vet, it turned out she was in crisis. She had pneumonia, fleas, ear mites, a matted coat, and the list goes on. The Adopt-A-Pet Shop dipped into their emergency fund and took care of nursing Faith back to health, for which we, and I'm sure the people who eventually adopted her on Nov. 1, 2014, are grateful!

We printed copies of this book via Amazon's Create Space and are donating 100 percent of the money earned through sales to The Adopt-A-Pet Shop. Thank you very much for the work you do to save cats like Faith, Stripes, Arthur and Anna!

The
Adopt
-A- Pet
Shop
8
OPEN

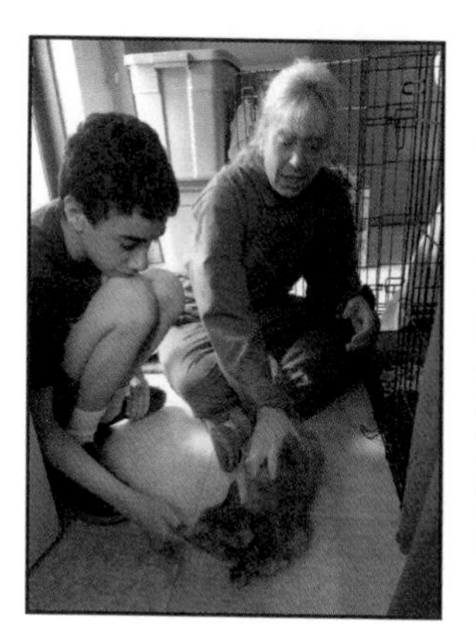

RESOURCES

According to the American Society for the Prevention of Cruelty to Animals (ASPCA)…

* Approximately 3.4 million cats enter animal shelters nationwide every year.

* Of the cats entering shelters, approximately 37% are adopted, 41% are euthanized and less than 5% who come in as strays are returned to their owners.

* 1.3 million cats are adopted each year.

* 1.4 million cats are euthanized each year.

* More than 35% of cats are acquired as strays.

* Many strays are lost pets who were not kept properly indoors or provided with identification.

According to the Humane Society of the United States…

* There are 95.6 million owned cats in the United States.

* 26% of owned cats were adopted from an animal shelter.

* The average amount of money cat owners spend on routine vet visits is $193 annually.

* 91% of owned cats are spayed or neutered.

Stripes

Caroline

Made in the USA
Charleston, SC
17 June 2015

Ladies on Fire Ministries
93 Camberwell Station Road
London, England SE5 9JJ
www.ladiesonfire.org
Email: drjennifer@ladiesonfire.org
Tel: 44 207 738 3668 (UK)
Tel: 1 347 708 1449 (USA)

How To Take Communion At Home

Dr. Jennifer Wiseman

CONTENTS

Introduction 9
The First Communion 12
From Passover to Communion 14
Communion In The Early Church 16
Self-Examination 18
Power of Communion 21
Seven Supernatural Blessings of Communion 23
Miracles of Communion 26
Smith Wigglesworth – God's General 30
Take Communion During The Storms of Life 35
Priesthood 37
Who Was Melchizedek? 39
The Two Tables 41
Forgiveness Is A Must Before Taking Communion 43
Can I Take Communion At Home? 45
Praying The Psalms After Communion 50
Questions & Answers 52

ACKNOWLEDGEMENTS

I give all the glory to my Father God of our Lord Jesus Christ for everything. For His wisdom, empowerment and revelation knowledge, to give me such a message at a time like this.

My deepest love and appreciation to my husband Bishop Climate, who is my pastor, my Bishop, my friend, my coach, my mentor and my prayer partner, and who has been a great encourager all through.

To my precious ones; Summer, so confident, I always love you. I'm proud of you girl for you are a mighty beautiful woman of God. Thank you for telling me and helping me in this book. Climate II Junior, my boy so sweet, tender, brave, strong, anointed youth-preacher. I thank you for your help in this book. Grace, beautiful and adorable, I thank you for your support in helping my book to come forth. Lastly but not least, my Baby Sunshine, beautiful, adorable, cute and gifted in her own ways. It's like you understand, even at only one years old, you were so quiet and freed me to write this book in a unique way. I thank you kids for giving me a space and allowing me to write this book.

My most sincere appreciation to all Ladies on Fire committees, you have been a source of encouragement, strength and inspiration. Thank you for standing with me to see this message go to the whole world.

My most sincere appreciation to all our TKC pastors, ministers, leaders, precious members and partners worldwide for your fellowship and believing in the vision God has given to Bishop and I; it has really encouraged us both to go even more miles in our spiritual life.

To my precious intercessors that have been the most encouraging and praying non-stop to see this book as the answer to all women in the world. Thank you so much, God bless you!

FOREWORD

Communion is one the most powerful and exhilarating commodities Jesus has given to the church. It is a reminder of the power of our redemption and activates healing and deliverance in our lives on a major and immeasurable scale. Dr. Jennifer has so exquisitely captured this principle in this easy to read and understandable book. Once you start to read it, you will not put it down, as God's healing power begins to work in your body, your mind and engage your spirit! Oh, what power you are going to experience through this book. Powerful, prevalent and amazing changes are waiting for you! Thank you, Dr. Jennifer, for this dynamic and anointed book!

From Apostle Helen Saddler
Into His Chambers
Seattle, WA

Dr. Jennifer is my friend and co-worker in the Lord's vineyard. A great preacher and writer in many books. But this particular book I'd say is an eye opener. It's full of information on how we the church have forgotten a very powerful tool that was practiced in the early church but now Dr. Jennifer has the mantle to bring this glory back to us believers. I must say it's a well written book, straight forward and easy to understand. Am really excited looking forward to the day it's available on Amazon.

From Bishop Deborah Bolton USA.
Heart of God Ministry

I recommend this to anyone who is a prayer warrior, those who think they aren't and those who are wondering why the Blood of Jesus is still so Powerful today!! This is your daily book and a mighty move of God will take place in your ministry. I call this book big revival. Dr. Jennifer, well done servant of God.

From Bishop Princess Hackman UK.

Beneficial Veracious Christ church

I'm a woman of God, on fire for Jesus.
I'm a fruitful vine within my house,
I have wisdom of God.
I'm a woman of integrity, clothed with God's strength.
I have hunger and thirst to sit at the feet of Jesus.
I'm rooted and grounded in the love of God,
With my light shining bright.
I'm a woman loosed, Satan is no longer my master, sin is no longer my master, sickness is no longer my master, fear is no longer my master, bondage of any kind is no longer my master.
Jesus has set me free; I'm on Fire For Jesus Christ.

Now before you continue, remember to put on the full armor of God according to Ephesians 6:10-18, touching each part of your body as you say it.

Repeat with me: "I put on the full armor of God. The helmet of salvation upon my head, the breastplate of righteousness in its place, the belt of truth around my waist, my feet shod with the readiness of the gospel of peace, taking the shield of faith in my left hand and the sword of the spirit in my right, which is the Word of God".

ONE

Introduction

I was raised up and have spent all my life in church. Growing up in Kenya, my parents were very devoted Catholics. As far as I can remember, my family participated in every church activity that took place. And I loved it. I loved being in church every day; I especially loved when I would attend all the services of the day just so that I could take the communion more than once. Every Sunday we had three services. There was a very early one for the early risers, another one was held in the local language or mother tongue, and finally a third mass was held in Swahili, our national language. I would make sure that I went to all three just so I could take part in all three communions. And though at the time I did not yet understand the power of it, I did revere it so much as we were taught to do.

I never ever complained about going to church or staying after service even if other meetings would take very long. Growing up I had more responsibility on my shoulders to help in and out of the church with my other sisters. We loved to help a lot. We were responsible for arranging many things before the mass started. Most of my family were in the choir groups, others were in youth groups and my sister Susan was the best reader of the scriptures almost every Sunday.

I knew everything and anything that was represented in the altar. But growing up in the Catholic church, my experience with communion was much different than what it was after I got born again. From the priest down to the little child, receiving the communion was no joke. During that time, you could not hear a single sound. There was no going out of service or coming in. Everybody was very calm during this special time. And it was done faithfully every single week.

But when I got born again, the church that I attended only took communion once a month. And even when we did take communion, it was nothing like I experienced as a child. Clearly the fear and reverence that I grew up practicing was fading away. As a result, I thought that it must not be important once you get born again as they did not place much emphasis on it.

That is until one day God showed me the amazing power of communion. When my daughter Summer was turning one, we were planning a big birthday party for her with a lot of family and friends. But she suddenly became very ill. She wasn't eating or playing with any of her toys. We prayed and we confessed the Word of God and her temperature improved but she was still very ill.

Then my husband told me that God spoke to him that we need to take communion in our home. At first, I was puzzled. I thought only a priest could minister communion to us. Furthermore how could a little child take communion? But he explained what to do and I said okay. We quickly prepared what we had in the house that day, some Ribena to drink and normal bread. That day we also had a family friend over who had brought along their 9 year old son, Onesimus. So I prepared four cups of juice and four pieces of bread for all of us.

The most amazing thing happened next. After taking the communion, our daughter was instantly healed. All the sickness left, she became well and began to play with her toys again which she had not touched all day long. Even my friend's son was surprised to witness what happened.

When the boy returned back to his home he shared with his mother what had happened and what he saw and how communion is very powerful. They also took communion and prayed for a better house and after exactly two weeks they got a bigger better house where Onesimus had his own big furnished bedroom. Hallelujah!

My friend I want you to join me in this book as I reveal to you how Communion can be taken not only in your church, but how you can make it a part of your daily life at home.

This was practiced regularly in the early church but today it's hardly ever done in believer's homes. I believe God has given me this mantle to bring it back into the homes of believers again so that God can do mighty miracles in their lives.

There were four things that the early church devoted themselves to; apostle's teaching, fellowship, prayer and communion. As a result they grew more and more and were healed and restored. I pray that these same blessings begin to be experienced in your life as well.

> And they steadfastly persevered, devoting themselves constantly to the instruction and fellowship of the apostles, to the breaking of bread [including the Lord's Supper] and prayers.
>
> (Acts 2:42)

TWO

The First Communion

> Then Melchizedek king of Salem brought out bread and wine. He was priest of God Most High, and he blessed Abram, saying, "Blessed be Abram by God Most High, Creator of heaven and earth. And praise be to God Most High, who delivered your enemies into your hand."
>
> (Genesis 14:18-20 NIV)

The very first communion was experienced by Abraham. The Bible tells us that Abraham travelled to Salem (now Jerusalem) to a valley later known as the Kidron valley where he met a priest called Melchizedek who served as king of Jerusalem and priest of God. He brought forth communion and pronounced blessings upon Abraham.

Years later, God asked Abraham to return to the same place to offer his son Isaac in the land of Moriah. The land of Moriah was the same area where Melchizedek blessed Abraham and had communion.

Those who have been to the Holy Land can testify of this. Those in our church who have travelled with us will remember when Archbishop Climate showed us and explained how this place was just across where the Lamb of God was crucified.

THREE

From Passover to Communion

The prophetic fulfilment of Passover is well narrated in the books of Jesus' disciples Matthew and Luke, the night that they shared the last supper with Jesus. Remember he told them go and prepare a place for Passover.

> Jesus sent Peter and John, saying, "Go and make preparations for us to eat the Passover."
>
> (Luke 22:8)

For the three years since Jesus began his ministry, he had been celebrating the Passover meal together with his disciples. Every year they celebrated it the same, but that night it took a turn.

When it came to that moment of eating the Passover bread, everything changed. Jesus made a powerful statement that no one had ever heard since the Israelites were freed from the land of bondage.

> Jesus took bread, and when he had given thanks, he broke it and gave it to his disciples, saying, "Take and eat; this is my body."
>
> (Matthew 26:26)

Wow! Here we see a transmission or transfer taking place. Suddenly the Passover meal now becomes the body of Jesus and the same with the blood of the lamb, it becomes Jesus' blood. Hallelujah!

PROPHETIC FULFILMENT OF PASSOVER

> Now the Festival of Unleavened Bread, called the Passover, was approaching, When the hour came, Jesus and his apostles reclined at the table. And he said to them, "I have eagerly desired to eat this Passover with you before I suffer. For I tell you, I will not eat it again until it finds fulfillment in the kingdom of God."
>
> (Luke 22:1,14-16 NIV)

This is a big mystery that the church has not discovered until now. It was the Final Passover that Jesus shared with his disciples where He made a transition from Passover to Communion. He was fulfilling the Passover feast that Jews have celebrated since they came out of Egypt (Exodus 14).

Passover is a great memorable day where God's people remember their freedom from Egypt and their future inheritance of the promise land. I believe Jesus fulfilled the old covenant Passover for shadowing this new covenant of communion.

So communion is our reminder today of our redemption through Christ's suffering and of our future inheritance with Christ in heaven.

FOUR

Communion In The Early Church

> And they continued steadfastly in the apostles' doctrine and fellowship, and in breaking of bread, and in prayers.
>
> (Acts 2:42 KJV)

The Bible tells us that the early church continued in four things, mainly the apostle's teaching, fellowship, prayer and communion.

After Jesus ascended to heaven, the early church continued practicing the Lord's Supper and it is referred to in particular by Paul in 1 Corinthians 11:23-26 in what have come to be called 'the words of institution'.

> For I received from the Lord what I also passed on to you: The Lord Jesus, on the night he was betrayed, took bread, and when he had given thanks, he broke it and said, "This is my body, which is for you; do this in remembrance of me." In the same way, after supper he took the cup, saying, "This cup is the new covenant in my blood; do this, whenever you drink it, in remembrance of

> me." For whenever you eat this bread and drink this cup, you proclaim the Lord's death until he comes.

This gives us a glimpse into the way communion was shaped in early times.

The Lord's Supper has past, present and future dimensions.

The bread and wine are symbols that the Son of God became flesh and blood and, in that humanity, offered himself as an atoning sacrifice upon the cross. He is indeed the 'Lamb of God who takes away the sin of the world!' (John 1:29).

Communion is therefore based upon an historical event which is deemed to have significance for the whole world. In Christ, God has done something that transforms the human situation and opens up a way of access to God. Communion points to this and is a continual reminder of it. The Lord's Supper proclaims the historical reality that Christ has come.

It has a future dimension because it anticipates a future reality of the coming Christ. When Jesus broke bread with his disciples, he told them,

> For I tell you that I will not eat it again until it is fulfilled in the kingdom of God."
>
> (Luke 22:16)

FIVE

Self-Examination

> For I received from the Lord what I also passed on to you: The Lord Jesus, on the night he was betrayed, took bread, and when he had given thanks, he broke it and said, "This is my body, which is for you; do this in remembrance of me." In the same way, after supper he took the cup, saying, "This cup is the new covenant in my blood; do this, whenever you drink it, in remembrance of me." For whenever you eat this bread and drink this cup, you proclaim the Lord's death until he comes.
>
> (1 Corinthians 11:23-26 NIV)

Taking the communion is not a joke or house routine but a very special meal with great honour to Almighty God. When taking communion you should know it's the Lord's blood and His body. There is a process in order to self-check yourself.

> Everyone ought to examine themselves before they eat of the bread and drink from the cup.
>
> (1 Corinthians 11:28 NIV)

1. Inward self-examination

This is like a spiritual X-ray, examining or looking for a result from your inner heart, mind and spirit. Ensure there is no hidden or known sin in your heart. Confess and ask God for forgiveness. From the heart flow all the issues of life, so the heart is the factory of all sin.

> Keep thy heart with all diligence; for out of it *are* the issues of life.
>
> (Proverbs 4:23)

Jesus said that it's what comes out of a man's mouth (his heart) that defiles a person.

> Keep thy heart with all diligence; for out of it *are* the issues of life.
>
> (Matthew 15:11)

If your heart senses guilt, repent and ask God for forgiveness immediately before taking communion at home. This action will keep you humble before God and pure in mind and spirit. This results in you leading a healthier, happier life.

2. Outward Self-examination

Looking or searching outward for any strife, malice, misunderstandings or disagreement between you and another person, family member or fellow believer. This straightens your relationship with others around you. Life is not always on your favour and sometimes you will disagree to agree with another.

Outward self-examination deals with reconciliation. If Christ forgave us then we should forgive others.

> Therefore, if you are offering your gift at the altar and there remember that your brother or sister has something against you, leave your gift there in front of the altar. First go and be reconciled to them; then come and offer your gift.
>
> (Matthew 5:23-24 NIV)

3. Upward self-examination

> Looking unto Jesus the author and finisher of our faith; who for the joy that was set before him endured the cross, despising the shame, and is set down at the right hand of the throne of God.
>
> (Hebrews 12:2 KJV)

Search upward and see His goodness, love and mercy to all of us, His mankind.

4. Onward self-examination

Looking forward to a long life and expectation of your fulfilled God-given purpose. Each one of us are created for a purpose.

> With long life will I satisfy him, and shew him my salvation.
>
> (Psalm 91:16 KJV)

SIX

Power of Communion

There are many powerful evidences that communion will produce in your life, but let's just mention four of them that will help you to become a powerful force against the enemy's camp. This sacred practice is often overlooked as an opportunity to release God's power in your life!

Don't settle for a lifeless routine. God is supernaturally present in the holy Communion! We as believers must learn to embrace these prophetic acts of worship, warfare, healing and deliverance as it was always meant to be.

When Jesus died He said it's finished so now you can take back everything that was stolen away from you. It's a done deal, He has paid the price for you.

1. Worship

Communion enables you to experience new dimensions of God's glory as you apply Jesus' victory over your life.

2. Warfare

Communion shifts spiritual atmospheres over you, your family and even world events around you.

3. Healing

Communion releases the healing testimony of Jesus' blood and body over sickness in our lives.

4. Deliverance

Communion announces the eternal victory of Jesus over torment, addiction and bondage in our lives.

SEVEN

Seven Supernatural Blessings of Communion

When God chose Abraham, He commanded him to leave his father's house and go to a land that He would show him. God called Abraham to bless him just as He called you and me. We too must obey His voice so that our families and those around us and connected to us will forever be blessed.

The Bible tells us that Abraham experienced a great favor from God, that God himself came down to bless him in the valley, bringing bread and wine. To me that's nothing else but communion. Abraham shared communion with Jesus first before anyone else. And from him we can see the seven supernatural benefits that we can expect as a result of communion.

1. Peace

> And Melchizedek king of Salem brought forth bread and wine: and he was the priest of the most high God. And he blessed him, and said, Blessed be Abram of the most high God, possessor of heaven and earth (Genesis 14:18-19 KJV)

Salem means peace. As Abraham took communion with Melchizedek the peace of God was flowing into his life.

2. Divine Blessing

Abraham was blessed by Melchizedek immediately after taking communion.

> And he blessed him, and said, Blessed be Abram of the most high God, possessor of heaven and earth. The word blessed means empowered to prosper and have a good success in everything he will do.
>
> (Genesis 14:19)

3. A Word from God

The word that you need will show up.

> After these things the word of the Lord came unto Abram in a vision, saying, Fear not, Abram: I am thy shield, and thy exceeding great reward.
>
> (Genesis 15:1 KJV)

4. Deliverance From Fear

> After these things the word of the Lord came unto Abram in a vision, saying, Fear not, Abram: I am thy shield, and thy exceeding great reward.
>
> (Genesis 15:1 KJV)

5. Supernatural Protection

> After these things the word of the Lord came unto Abram in a vision, saying, Fear not, Abram: I am thy shield, and thy exceeding great reward.
>
> (Genesis 15:1 KJV)

6. Supernatural Provision

God will be to you an exceeding great reward.

> After these things the word of the Lord came unto Abram in a vision, saying, Fear not, Abram: I am thy shield, and thy exceeding great reward.
>
> (Genesis 15:1 KJV)

7. The Impossible Is Made Possible

> Is anything too hard for the Lord? At the time appointed I will return unto thee, according to the time of life, and Sarah shall have a son.
>
> (Genesis 18:14 KJV)

EIGHT

Miracles of Communion

In the Old Testament, during the very first Passover, God instructed the children of Israel to eat unleavened bread and slaughter and eat their sacrificial lamb, both symbolic of the body and blood of Jesus, just like during Communion. We cannot deny or forget the incredible miracles that took place in the time of Passover in Exodus. But the secret I want to share with you is that you can expect the same kind of miracles after taking communion and applying the Blood of Jesus to your life.

Oh yes, that night after taking their instructed meal the Israelites began experiencing mighty miracles. Their boss (the Egyptians) gave them jewels, gold and so much from their treasures.

From the least to the greatest, they were all given unusual strength to make the journey. Not one of them was sick or weak. God opened the Red Sea for them so that they could cross over easily, at the same time killing all their enemies. And for all that time of wandering in the desert, their clothes and shoes never wore out. Day after day they experienced divine provision in the wilderness with manna from heaven and water pouring out of rocks.

When you begin to understand the power behind communion and make it a regular part of your life, God takes care of you in unusual ways. He will up open doors for you that the world can't figure it out. Yes as you take communion you will encounter supernatural provision in every area of life.

But not just that! When the children of Israel slaughtered their lamb it was symbolic of them applying the Blood of Jesus to their lives, just like Communion. And look at what happened as a result:

The Blood of the Lamb delivered the Israelites from 400 years of Egyptian bondage.

The Blood of the Lamb made the Angel of death pass over them and supernaturally protected their first born from death.

The Blood of the Lamb put a distinction mark between God's people and their enemy.

The Blood of the Lamb healed the sick.

The Blood of the Lamb provided supernatural miracles that their shoes never wore out for 40 years.

As you begin to take Communion, that Holy Balanced Meal, the Bread and Blood of Jesus will supernaturally strengthen, deliver, heal and restore you.

The Mystery of His Blood

When Adam and Eve sinned in the garden, God killed the first lamb, symbolic of the Lamb of God that would come and take away the sin of the world.

When God was getting ready to bring the children of Israel out of Egypt, he commanded them to take one lamb for each family and kill it, spreading its blood over their doorpost so that when God saw it He would pass over; the spirit of death would not visit the home upon which the lamb's blood was placed. Since then, the Israelites continued this practice of

Passover every year, each family bringing their sacrificial lamb to the priest to be slaughtered and atone for their sins.

My question is, how could the blood of a little lamb have such authority over death?

Better yet, how can the blood of one man, Jesus Christ have such power over the enemy?

What is so special about the blood of Jesus Christ?

When God created man in his own image, he breathed life into his nostrils the breath of life and became a living soul.

> Then the LORD God formed a man from the dust of the ground and breathed into his nostrils the breath of life, and the man became a living being. (Genesis 2:7)

The Bible tells us that the life of the body is in the blood.

> For the life of the body is in its blood.
>
> (Leviticus 17:11)

Inside Jesus' blood contains Divine life, flowing from God to us. Hallelujah. His DNA has the blood of Almighty God, our Father.

When God created man in the garden of Eden, he placed inside of him a living substance that satan nor the angels had even seen before. It was the blood. Remember, angels are spirits without physical bodies, they don't have blood in their bodies. But you and I are a spirit with a physical body. So when we take in the blood of Jesus, it mysteriously begins to change everything inside of us.

Angels had never known of blood until the creation of Adam. I imagine them questioning each other. What is this? God has given His precious blood that carries His life, His peace, His joy, His kindness, His righteousness, His holiness, I can go on and on amen.

Blood Has A Voice

When Cain killed Abel his brother, the Bible says that his blood spoke from the ground.

> Then the Lord said to Cain, "Where is your brother Abel?" "I don't know," he replied. "Am I my brother's keeper?" The Lord said, "What have you done? Listen! Your brother's blood cries out to me from the ground.
>
> (Genesis 4:9-10)

Blood has a voice. Abel's blood was not only speaking of what his brother Cain had done but also speaking of revenge for all the future children and descendants from Abel's loins that would no longer walk the earth. Cain didn't just destroy Abel but all of his descendants as well.

So blood has a voice. Yes blood can speak to God. Even when you are dead your blood speaks. If this is true for just mere humans, then what about the precious blood of Jesus?

> By faith Abel offered unto God a more excellent sacrifice than Cain, by which he obtained witness that he was righteous, God testifying of his gifts: and by it he being dead yet speaketh.
>
> (Hebrews 11:4 KJV)

> To Jesus the mediator of a new covenant, and to the sprinkled blood that speaks a better word than the blood of Abel.
>
> (Hebrews 12:24 NIV)

The blood of Jesus speaks better than the blood of Abel. After you take communion, the blood of Jesus in your body speaks healing, speaks restoration and everything else that Jesus died for you to have.

NINE

Smith Wigglesworth – God's General

Smith Wigglesworth was born on 8 June 1859 in Menston, Yorkshire, England, to an impoverished family. As a small child, he worked in the fields pulling turnips alongside his mother; he also worked in factories to help provide for his family. He was illiterate as a child because of his labors.

Nominally a Methodist, he became a born-again Christian at the age of eight. His grandmother was a devout Methodist; his parents, John and Martha, took young Smith to Methodist and Anglican churches on regular occasions. He was confirmed by a Bishop in the Church of England, baptized by immersion in the Baptist Church and had the grounding in Bible teaching in the Plymouth Brethren while learning the plumbing trade as an apprentice from a man in the Brethren movement.

His Family

Wigglesworth married Polly Featherstone on 2 May 1882. At the time of their marriage, she was a preacher with the Salvation Army and had come to the attention of General

William Booth. They had one daughter, Alice, and four sons, Seth, Harold, Ernest and George. His grandson, Leslie Wigglesworth, after more than 20 years as a missionary in the Congo, served as the president of the Elim Pentecostal Church.

His Wife Taught Him To Read The Bible

Wigglesworth learned to read after he married Polly; she taught him to read the Bible. He often stated that it was the only book he ever read, and did not permit newspapers in his home, preferring the Bible to be their only reading material.

Wigglesworth worked as a plumber, but he abandoned this trade because he was too busy for it after he started preaching. In 1907, Wigglesworth visited Alexander Boddy during the Sunderland Revival, and following a laying-on of hands from Alexander's wife, Mary Boddy, he experienced speaking in tongues. He spoke at some of the Assemblies of God events in Great Britain. He also received ministerial credentials with the Assemblies of God in the United States, where he evangelized during the 1920s and later.

His Ministry

Wigglesworth believed that healing came through faith, and he was flexible in his approach. When he was forbidden to lay hands on audience members by the authorities in Sweden, he preached for a "corporate healing", by which people laid hands on themselves. He also practiced anointing with oil, and the distribution of "prayer handkerchiefs" (one of which was sent to King George V). Wigglesworth sometimes attributed ill-health to demons.

Smith largely believed his ministerial success was due to his speaking in tongues. He said:

"I want you to see that he that speaketh in an unknown tongue edifieth himself or builds himself up. We must be edified before we can edify the church. I cannot estimate what I, personally, owe to the Holy Ghost method of spiritual edification. I am here before you as one of the biggest conundrums in the world. There never was a weaker man on the platform. Language? None. Inability–full of it. All natural things in my life point exactly opposite to my being able to stand on the platform and preach the gospel. The secret is that the Holy Ghost came and brought this wonderful edification of the Spirit. I had been reading this Word continually as well as I could, but the Holy Ghost came and took hold of it, for the Holy Ghost is the breath of it, and He illuminated it to me."

His Daily Communion At Home

My family and I follow the same plan Smith Wigglesworth had. We start every morning with Communion together. Some days we discover other tables He leads us to - on the streets, in restaurants, coffee houses, hospitals... we never know but we are ready! We carry Bread, Cups and 'Wine' in a carry bag at all times.

Do you want a powerful key to success in your life, your relationships, your business, your mission? Start the day by being with Him and watch what happens when His presence is fresh in your life every day. He is there smiling & waiting for you. He is always there and wants to be with you. Discover the Miracle of Communion Fire. It is being with Jesus through the bread and wine... everyday!

The Hour Is Come

Smith Wigglesworth lived in this modern Pentecostal view. Holy Communion was very special and important to Him. It was part of his daily walk with God. George Stormont writes of Wigglesworth, "He did this every day [take Holy Communion] whether he was home or not. If other believers were with him, he would share with them. If not, he would partake alone." (George Stormont, Wigglesworth: A Man Who Walked With God, Harrison House, Tulsa, 1989, p. 77.)

It is against this background that Wigglesworth in December 1929 did his teaching on Holy Communion in "The Hour Is Come." For Wigglesworth, Holy Communion was not to be a morose meditation upon the suffering of Jesus; it was, rather, to be seen as a moment of unveiling His glory by the sealing of a New Covenant with God the Father that would make the fullness of divine life available to all who believe in Christ.

Wigglesworth once mentioned that early in his ministry he had a vision of Jesus standing by the cross. Jesus instructed Wigglesworth to always remember that although He had gone to the cross for him, He (Jesus) was no longer on the cross but on the throne at the right hand of God the Father. Wigglesworth was instructed by Christ to see Him as Lord, ruling and reigning in power, a power which was fully available to Wigglesworth if he would have faith.

Wigglesworth brings this same "theology of glory" to his teaching on Holy Communion. For Wigglesworth, partaking of the bread and the cup is to be a radical saying "Yes" to the fullness of divine life and power that is available to us through Christ. When we eat the earthly bread and drink the earthly cup, we are looking beyond these earthly symbols and we embrace the true bread, which has come down from heaven, and is given for the life of the world (John 6:48-51).

I really enjoyed this Gods general walk of faith. I was so excited searching his life especially with communion. He has done so many but I have to stay focused on communion. It's recorded that He raised many from the dead and in his conferences amazing unforgettable healings took place.

Just like Smith Wigglesworth, enjoy communion at home or office in the fullness of what our Lord wants for you every time you remember Him in Holy Communion. Amen.

TEN

Take Communion During The Storms of Life

As you have been reading my book, if you or anyone you know is going through a storm in their life, invite them to take communion and pass this message to them and I guarantee you soon their miracle will happen.

Communion will bring you out safely from any form of storm, challenge or difficulty in your life. After taking communion the children of Israel passed through the Red Sea miraculously despite Pharaoh and his army being so close to them. They also crossed through the wilderness miraculously with supernatural provision of food and divine protection from beasts.

> He led you through the vast and dreadful wilderness, that thirsty and waterless land, with its venomous snakes and scorpions. He brought you water out of hard rock.
>
> (Deuteronomy 8:15)

In the book of Acts 27, Paul warned the sailors before they left that a storm was coming, but they didn't heed his warning. In the middle of their journey while they were at sea, a strong storm hit their boat just like Paul said. But Paul stood up and encouraged them, telling them how the night before an angel of the Lord stood by him and assured him they would make it to the other side but they would lose their boat and cargo. Paul then took communion right there in the midst of the storm.

> After he said this, he took some bread and gave thanks to God in front of them all. Then he broke it and began to eat.
>
> (Acts 27:35)

Let this be an encouragement when you are facing the storms of life. They don't need to overcome you when you take communion. When you are facing a financial storm, take communion. When you are facing a marriage storm, take communion. Your victory is guaranteed.

ELEVEN

Priesthood

At this point you might have a lot of questions in your mind. Like who will lead the communion in your home. Well you may not be a pastor or a priest, but you don't need to be. As long as you are born again you can lead yourself or your family or your colleagues at work in taking communion without any doubt.

This was a huge eye-opener for me when I finally realized it. Because I grew up in the Catholic church I thought that only the priest could perform this special ceremony. So the day when my husband told me he could lead the communion in our home, I thought he was making a mistake. But watching our daughter recover before our very eyes, I knew it was true.

You Are The Priest To Lead Communion At Home

At home, fathers are the head of the family. Father's should take charge to lead the family in breaking the bread at home. It is so powerful because the devil can't stand it to see the man or father taking charge. God has chosen him as his priest. But if the father is not at home or around, then the mother, sons or daughters can break the bread at home as well. As long as you are saved.

God Has Made You A Priest

> And from Jesus Christ, who is the faithful witness, the firstborn from the dead, and the ruler of the kings of the earth. To him who loves us and has freed us from our sins by his blood, and has made us to be a kingdom and priests to serve his God and Father---to him be glory and power for ever and ever! Amen. (Revelation 1:5-6)

You Are A Royal Race, Chosen People, Priesthood, Holy Nation, Gods Special Possession

But you are a chosen people, a royal priesthood, a holy nation, God's special possession, that you may declare the praises of him who called you out of darkness into his wonderful light. (1 Peter 2:9)

Yes, He made us to be a kingdom and priest to serve our God and Father. To him be glory and power for ever and ever. Amen. Remember it's not just kings and priests, but He has made us a kingdom of priests

> Now if you obey me fully and keep my covenant, then out of all nations you will be my treasured possession. Although the whole earth is mine, you will be for me a kingdom of priests and a holy nation.' These are the words you are to speak to the Israelites. (Exodus 19:5-6 NIV)

TWELVE

Who Was Melchizedek?

As we read at the beginning, in the book of Genesis 14 a powerful event took place at Kidron Valley between Abraham and Melchizedek, king of Salem and priest. He brought forth communion and pronounced blessings upon Abraham.

> Then Melchizedek king of Salem brought out bread and wine. He was priest of God Most High, and he blessed Abram, saying, "Blessed be Abram by God Most High, Creator of heaven and earth. And praise be to God Most High, who delivered your enemies into your hand." Then Abram gave him a tenth of everything. (Genesis 14:18-20 NIV)

But who was this Melchizedek?

> This Melchizedek was king of Salem and priest of God Most High. He met Abraham returning from the defeat of the kings and blessed him, and Abraham gave him a tenth of everything. First, the name Melchizedek means "king of righteousness"; then also, "king of Salem" means "king of peace." Without father or mother, without genealogy, without beginning of days or end of life,

resembling the Son of God, he remains a priest forever. (Hebrews 7:2-3)

His name means King of Righteousness and King of Peace. He had no physical father or mother, he had no beginning of days or end of life. This was Jesus manifesting in the Old Testament in the form of Melchizedek.

The moment you take communion, you will experience peace inside of you. For you are partaking of the King of Peace. So it doesn't matter what is against you, He will meet you at the communion table in a miraculous way.

THIRTEEN

The Two Tables

The other day I was thinking about our dining table at home, how we value it and treasure it. How it has to be cleaned and organized every time. Especially when we are about to take a family meal; everything is arranged systematically.

The Table Of The Lord Is Dispersed

In the book of Malachi, it pains me to hear God talking about His meal table being dispersed, disrespected, and dishonored by us offering polluted bread.

> Ye offer polluted bread upon mine altar; and ye say, Wherein have we polluted thee? In that ye say, The table of the Lord is contemptible.
>
> (Malachi 1:7 KJV)

> "By offering defiled food on my altar. "But you ask, 'How have we defiled you?' "By saying that the Lord's table is contemptible.
>
> (Malachi 1:7 NIV)

Although God is speaking of what we offer to Him but at the same time about communion.

One day God spoke to me in a dream about two tables. One table was of the Lord and another table was of demons. When I woke up, I quickly checked these scriptures describing the two tables.

> Is not the cup of thanksgiving for which we give thanks a participation in the blood of Christ? And is not the bread that we break a participation in the body of Christ? You cannot drink the cup of the Lord and the cup of demons too; you cannot have a part in both the Lord's table and the table of demons.
>
> (1 Corinthians 10:16, 21)

> Be ye not unequally yoked together with unbelievers: for what fellowship hath righteousness with unrighteousness? and what communion hath light with darkness?
>
> (2 Corinthians 6:14 KJV)

Communion comes from the Greek word koinonia meaning partnership or participation; communication.

There are two kinds of tables, the Lord's table and the demon's table and both of them have a purpose to share life.

The Lord's table is God himself sharing His life, divine joy, divine peace in Him, and this is all through communion.

But the demon's table is demons sharing satan's evil wish with you, manifesting in sin, sickness and all kinds of evil.

Demons participate in demon's tables over your life and your dear ones. If you find you have a problem that won't go away or the same problems keep coming back again and again it's because in this demons table they are sharing demon's life where you are concerned.

FOURTEEN

Forgiveness Is A Must Before Taking Communion

As I mentioned earlier, we must examine ourselves before taking communion. Part of that self-examination involves the willful choice we make to forgive others as Christ forgave us. Jesus willingly shed his blood and his body to be bruised and crucified.

Before communion I first give thanks to God for His power of redemption. Then I ask God to forgive me of all my sins I have done knowingly and unknowingly. Also I start self-examination and I confess any action, asking God to forgive me and cleanse me. I then proceed to search my heart, deeper and deeper and if I find anyone I know who has offended me, I release them.

Through self-examination, guilt, sin and bitterness will not remain in us. For God is a forgiving God.

> If we confess our sins, he is faithful and just and will forgive us our sins and purify us from all unrighteousness.
>
> (1 John 1:9)

Let a man examine himself because confession of sin is an agreement with God.

Don't allow any bitterness to rule or reign over you no matter how deeply you are hurt. Yes, they may have abandoned you, rejected you, talked about you, betrayed you, lied to you. But don't stay in bitterness.

Many sick people face this issue. The biggest problem is not what they are eating but what is eating them. At the same time, many are also sick not as a result of what they are eating but who they are eating!

> But if ye bite and devour one another, take heed that ye be not consumed one of another.
>
> (Galatians 5:15 KJV)

The Greek word for devour means "to eat down". They we're eating each other.

You need to choose to eat the communion rather than to make a diet of people you don't like, people who have betrayed you, relatives who despise you or people who have offended you. Just remember that Jesus Christ is the fresh manna bread from heaven of today.

> Whoso eateth my flesh, and drinketh my blood, hath eternal life; and I will raise him up at the last day. For my flesh is meat indeed, and my blood is drink indeed. He that eateth my flesh, and drinketh my blood, dwelleth in me, and I in him.
>
> (John 6:54-56 KJV)

FIFTEEN

Can I Take Communion At Home?

If this is the question you have been asking then I'm happy to tell you YES! A BIG YES! And that is one of the reasons why I wrote this book.

Here's what the Scriptures say about taking communion at home.

> They devoted themselves to the apostles' teaching and to fellowship, to the breaking of bread and to prayer. Everyone was filled with awe at the many wonders and signs performed by the apostles. All the believers were together and had everything in common. Every day they continued to meet together in the temple courts. They broke bread in their homes and ate together with glad and sincere hearts, praising God and enjoying the favor of all the people. And the Lord added to their number daily those who were being saved.
>
> (Acts 2:42-47 NIV)

When He had reclined *at the table* with them, He took the bread and blessed *it,* and breaking *it,* He *began* giving *it* to them. Then their eyes were opened and they recognized Him; and He vanished from their sight. They *began* to relate their experiences on the road and how He was recognized by them in the breaking of the bread.

(Luke 24:30-31, 35)

Examine Yourself Before Communion

Therefore whoever eats the bread or drinks the cup of the Lord in an unworthy manner, shall be guilty of the body and the blood of the Lord. But a man must examine himself, and in so doing he is to eat of the bread and drink of the cup.

(1 Cor 11: 27-29)

How do you examine yourself before taking communion? Ask the Holy Spirit to lead you. As I shared earlier, forgiveness is a must.

But in case it helps you, Let me share with you what I normally do when taking communion at home. When I kneel down to take the Lord's Supper, I follow this general sequence of events.

Prayer

1. Pray

First, I pray by welcoming and inviting Gods presence into our midst in my home and family.

2. Repent

Then I repent of any sin and confess it right away before Him. I also forgive anyone who have sinned against me by faith in Jesus name

3. Plea the Blood

Then I ask the Lord to cover me with His precious blood and fill me anew and afresh with His Spirit.

4. Look to Him

Then I focus my mind on Jesus the author and finisher of our faith especially what he did for me on Calvary because of his love.

5. Give Thanks

I thank Him for forgiving all of my sins and dying for me.

6. Recommit my life

Then I give my life to Him all over again and I begin to thank Him for His sacrifice that saved me from death and gave me eternal life with Him.

Communion

After praying, I will take Communion. I eat the bread/wafer and drink the grape juice (representing His body and blood). You can also buy the ready-made packets from any online or physical Bible/Christian Bookstore.

Read and Confess Scripture

Then I declare the Word of God on Communion from 1 Corinthians 11:23-26

> For I received from the Lord what I also passed on to you: The Lord Jesus, on the night he was betrayed, took bread, and when he had given thanks, he broke it and said, "This is my body, which is for you; do this in remembrance of me." In the same way, after supper he took the cup, saying,

> "This cup is the new covenant in my blood; do this, whenever you drink it, in remembrance of me." For whenever you eat this bread and drink this cup, you proclaim the Lord's death until he comes.
>
> (1 Corinthians 11:23-26 NIV)

Present Your Request

After this is when I present my requests to God. Here's an example of how I normally pray.

In the name of Jesus, I apply the blood and body of Jesus Christ into my life, the lives of my family, my children, my marriage, my mind, my finances, my ministry, my business and everything that pertains to me.

With the blood of Jesus and in the name of Jesus, I break every curse, every witchcraft and every enemy assigned against me or my family. I take authority over every evil thing, every evil place, every evil person surrounding my life. I command them to run away when no one pursue them in Jesus name. Away from my life, away from my family, away from my marriage in Jesus name.

And now I loose God's holy power of protection over me, over my family and over my loved ones and everything that pertains to us. I decree that my family and I and everything that pertains to us are hidden in the secret place of the Most High, for we dwell under the shadow of Almighty God.

Lord Jesus, loose Your holy flow, Your healing, resurrection life, joy, peace, righteousness, power, and Your perfect peace that is in your blood into my body, my mind and my destiny in your name now and forever. Amen."

Finish With Our Lord's Prayer

Finally I finish with the Lord's Prayer.

> 'Our Father in heaven, hallowed be your name. Your kingdom come, your will be done, on earth as it is in heaven. Give us this day our daily bread, and forgive us our debts, as we also have forgiven our debtors. And lead us not into temptation, but deliver us from evil.'
>
> (Matthew 6:9-13)

Remember the Early Church practiced communion daily in their homes and they experienced a mighty refreshing of God's power and miracles in their lives. Yet, somehow this practice has been lost and forgotten amongst today's believers. No wonder we're not experiencing the same flow of blessings like the early church did. So let's change that. Let's revive it back again, especially in our homes.

SIXTEEN

Praying The Psalms After Communion

There is one more thing I love to do after taking Communion, after I have finished everything and said the Lord's prayer, I will pray aloud Psalms 136. I encourage you to do it as well or any other psalms that speak to you. God will grant you victory.

> Give thanks to the Lord, for he is good. His love endures forever. Give thanks to the God of gods. His love endures forever. Give thanks to the Lord of lords: His love endures forever. to him who alone does great wonders, His love endures forever. who by his understanding made the heavens, His love endures forever. who spread out the earth upon the waters, His love endures forever. who made the great lights---His love endures forever. the sun to govern the day, His love endures forever. the moon and stars to govern the night; His love endures forever. to him who struck down the firstborn of Egypt His love endures forever. and brought Israel out from among them His love endures forever. with a mighty hand and outstretched arm; His love endures forever. to him who divided the Red Sea asunder His love endures forever. and brought Israel

through the midst of it, His love endures forever. but swept Pharaoh and his army into the Red Sea; His love endures forever. to him who led his people through the wilderness; His love endures forever. to him who struck down great kings, His love endures forever. and killed mighty kings---His love endures forever. Sihon king of the Amorites His love endures forever. and Og king of Bashan---His love endures forever. and gave their land as an inheritance, His love endures forever. an inheritance to his servant Israel. His love endures forever. He remembered us in our low estate His love endures forever. and freed us from our enemies. His love endures forever. He gives food to every creature. His love endures forever. Give thanks to the God of heaven. His love endures forever.

(Psalm 136:1-26 NIV)

SEVENTEEN

Questions & Answers

How many times can you take communion?

> For as often as ye eat this bread, and drink this cup, ye do shew the lord's death till he come. (1 Corinthians 11:26)

You can do it as often as you like, preferably every day or as it's needed. As you eat it you proclaim, preach, teach, speak of and declare what Jesus has done until your miracle comes.

It's your healing table
It's your deliverance table
It's your miracle table
It's your Jehovah Rapha table

Who is unworthy to take communion and what are the consequences?

As long as you are born again, you are entitled to take it. But communion is not for anyone and everybody.

> So then, whoever eats the bread or drinks the cup of the Lord in an unworthy manner will be guilty of sinning against the body and blood of the Lord. Everyone ought to

> examine themselves before they eat of the bread and drink from the cup. For those who eat and drink without discerning the body of Christ eat and drink judgment on themselves. That is why many among you are weak and sick, and a number of you have fallen asleep. (1 Corinthians 11:27-30)

Imagine how many people today are weak and sick in their bodies because they eat rubbish. They are not discerning the body of Christ when they eat and so they are eating and drinking judgement on themselves. Drinking it in an unworthily manner means taking it without the understanding that he died for you and taking it without reverence and fear of God.

Who is allowed to take communion?

Anyone that is saved or must be saved.

> And he said unto them, unto you it is given to know the mystery of the kingdom of god: but unto them that are without, all these things are done in parables. (Mark 4:11)

PERSONAL NOTE FROM THE AUTHOR

I want you to know how much I appreciate your support by buying this book and reading it. Because of you, I was assigned to bring this communion back to the body of Christ. Today many have forgotten the power of communion. Taking it at home is mostly unheard of and many and have to wait until the one Sunday a month where it is done at church. But I pray God will do something special for you as you begin to practise this at home.

I request you to get this word out there to many. Feel free to advertise my book on your social media to announce to as many as you can. The Bible says in Psalms 66:18 that you are great because of publishing or advertising the Gospel all over the world. Am looking forward to hear your test testimony.

Thanks again,

Dr. Jennifer

Ladies On Fire Ministries
93 Camberwell Station Road, London, SE5 9JJ
England, United Kingdom
Tel: +44 207 738 3668 (UK)
Tel: 1 347 708 1449 (USA)
Email: drjennifer@ladiesonfire.org

Yes Dr Jennifer! I want to come into agreement with you that as I sow this seed according to the number of my age I will receive a physical manifestation of powerful miracles in every area of my life.

£ ________ (Please also send me: Anointed Oil for Total Victory)

Here is my Prayer Request covering the 7 areas I would like the Lord to manifest His miracles in my life:

____
____
____
____
____
____
____
____
____
____
____
____
____
____

(Continued on Back)

Name:

____

Address:

____

____

____

____

____

____

____

Telephone:

____

Email:

____

ABOUT DR JENNIFER

First Lady of the Kingdom Church and President of Ladies on Fire, this is the woman of God behind the powerful, lifechanging ministry of The Kingdom Church and Bishop Climate Ministries. A powerful woman of God, anointed with extra-ordinary wisdom for women.

Dr. Jennifer is a devoted wife to Bishop Climate and a loving mother of four children. She epitomizes the virtuous woman mentioned in Proverbs 31. She is a constant source of love and support to Bishop, The Kingdom Church members and partners. She has committed herself to birth strength to all church members. Her humility, warmth and genuine love for God and people have led to her counselling and touching many lives. Her anointing towards women is incredible and continue bringing great healing and restoration to many through her ministry LADIES ON FIRE MINISTRY. She travels the world to speak to and empower women of all ages hosting a number of conventions each year in cities across the World. Many families, businesses and individuals around the world have been impacted by ladies on fire international conferences.

Dr. Jennifer's dynamic teaching style and practical approach to ministry have ministered to millions over the years on topics that range from Christian family and biblical prosperity to character development.

She has written 7 powerful best-selling books and is well known by her TV programs on Sky digital TV, Ladies on Fire 24 Internet TV, DVDs and audio CDs. Also known by her 3 phenomenal Ladies on Fire International Conferences in UK and Africa (Catch the Fire Conference, Unforgettable Woman Conference and Esther Banquet conference).

Why not join us at an upcoming conference in your area? Follow her on Facebook, Twitter and YouTube

drjennifer@bishopclimate.org
drjennifer@ladiesonfire.org
firstladytkc@yahoo.co.uk
www.bishopclimate.org
www.ladiesonfire.org
Tel: +44 01315552290
Tel: +44 02077383668

OTHER BOOKS BY THE AUTHOR

Power of Confession
How To Sanctify Your Home
21 Days Daniel Fasting
A-Z Women in the Bible
The Proverbs 31 Woman
Queens & Queen Mothers In The Bible
How To Take Communion At Home

To order more books or for more resources on Communion and taking it at home, please call our prayer line today.

Tel: +44 207 738 3668 (UK)
Tel: 1 347 708 1449 (USA)

Made in the USA
Las Vegas, NV
08 January 2024